In the Know

INFLUENCERS AND TRENDS

SNEAKERS

Virginia Loh-Hagan

45° 45TH PARALLEL PRESS

Published in the United States of America by Cherry Lake Publishing Group
Ann Arbor, Michigan
www.cherrylakepublishing.com

Reading Adviser: Marla Conn, MS, Ed., Literacy specialist, Read-Ability, Inc.
Book Designer: Felicia Macheske

Photo Credits: © Indigo Photo Club/Shutterstock, cover; © juhe-IdeeID/Shutterstock, cover, 1; © OKcamera/ shutterstock,1; © Vadim Kostin/shutterstock,1; © Iakov Filimonov/shutterstock, 4; © Africa Studio/shutterstock, 6; © Nao Novoa/shutterstock, 7; © LightField Studios/shutterstock, 8; © hurricanehank/shutterstock, 10; © Beauty Style/shutterstock, 12; © Nazar Skladanyi/shutterstock, 14; © Photology1971/shutterstock, 15; © DuxX/ shutterstock, 16; © andersphoto/shutterstock, 18; © Mohamad Kaddoura/Dreamstime, 20; © gmn/shutterstock, 22; © Albo/shutterstock, 23; © iJeab/shutterstock, 24; © Sausin/shutterstock,26; © insta_photos/shutterstock, 28; © Dmitriev Mikhail/shutterstock, 31

45th Parallel Press is an imprint of Cherry Lake Publishing Group.

Library of Congress Cataloging-in-Publication Data

Names: Loh-Hagan, Virginia, author.
Title: Sneakers / Virginia Loh-Hagan.
Description: Ann Arbor, Michigan : Cherry Lake Publishing, [2021] | Series:
In the know : Influencers and trends | Includes index. | Summary: "We're spilling
the tea on the latest trends. Curious about the lives of influencers? Want to know
more about sneaker culture or see-through sneakers? Read more to be in the know.
This high-interest series is written at a low readability to aid struggling readers. Each
book includes educational sidebars, throwback biographies of "OG" influencers, fast
facts, and social media challenges, as well as a table of contents, glossary of keywords,
index, and author biography"— Provided by publisher.
Identifiers: LCCN 2020032507 (print) | LCCN 2020032508 (ebook)
| ISBN 9781534180376 (hardcover) | ISBN 9781534182080 (paperback)
| ISBN 9781534181380 (pdf) | ISBN 9781534183094 (ebook)
Subjects: LCSH: Sneakers—Juvenile literature. | Fashion—Juvenile literature.
Classification: LCC GV749.S64 L64 2021 (print) | LCC GV749.S64 (ebook) |
DDC 685/.31—dc23
LC record available at https://lccn.loc.gov/2020032507
LC ebook record available at https://lccn.loc.gov/2020032508

Cherry Lake Publishing Group would like to acknowledge the work of the Partnership for 21st Century Learning, a Network of Battelle for Kids. Please visit *http://www.battelleforkids.org/networks/p21* for more information.

Printed in the United States of America
Corporate Graphics

Dr. Virginia Loh-Hagan is an author, university professor, and former classroom teacher.
She was influenced by Kate Middleton. She bought a pair of Superga white platform sneakers.
She lives in San Diego with her very tall husband and very naughty dogs. To learn more
about her, visit www.virginialoh.com.

Many people buy, sell, and trade
sneakers like stocks on the stock market.
Stocks are small pieces of a company.

Introduction

What's **trending**? What's in? What's not? Trends are popular fads. They're all the rage. They're widely talked about. They **dominate** the internet. Dominate means to rule over.

Influencers are people who set trends. They post a lot on **social media**. Social media are online communication platforms used to share information. Influencers post photos and videos. They post blogs and stories. They inspire a **following**. Following refers to fans. Fans make trends come to life. They spread trends. They make trends popular.

Some trends stick. Some trends don't. This book explores sneaker trends.

Sneakers are also called trainers, runners, kicks, or tennis shoes. They have rubber **soles**. Soles are shoe bottoms. Rubber makes the shoes quiet. Wearers can "sneak" around. That's why sneakers are called sneakers.

Sneakers are designed for sports. They have flexible soles. They have tread for grip. They can absorb impact. They're good for running, dancing, and jumping.

But today, sneakers are a fashion trend. Fashion means clothing styles. They're worn all day long. They're worn by all types of people. They're worn for different reasons. People wear them to school. They wear them to work. They wear them to parties. Sneakers are cool for any event.

The tread on sneakers was inspired by waffles. ▶

"Hypebeast" is what sneakerheads
call people who buy the latest
sneakers and fashion styles.

Sneakerheads

Sneakers come in all shapes and sizes. They're more than just shoes. They are a form of expression for many people. Sneakerheads are people who really love sneakers. They wear and collect sneakers. They trade sneakers. They talk about sneakers. They go to sneaker events. They know all about sneakers.

Sneakerhead culture formed in the 1980s. It was inspired by basketball and hip-hop music. Shoe companies made special sneakers. Some sneakers are rare. They have special colors. They have special styles. This inspired sneakerheads to start sneaker collections. Some sneaker collections are worth a lot of money. Collectibles are kept in great shape. They're never worn. They're kept in their boxes.

Mark "Mayor" Farese is a sneakerhead. He owns over 3,600 sneakers. His collection is worth more than $1 million! He said, "[Companies] want to give me a product, because they know I'm going to post it on social media or I'm going to wear it."

Vashtie is another well-known sneakerhead. She's a director, DJ, and designer. She's the first woman to design her own Jordan sneaker.

Benjamin Kapelushnik is known as "Benjamin Kickz." He has 1 million Instagram followers. He buys and sells sneakers. He sells to famous people. He started at age 12. He's made about $1 million. He did this before finishing high school.

◄ Sneaker culture was popularized by sports stars and musicians like Michael Jordan, Travis Scott, and Kanye West.

There are low and high platform
sneakers. High platform sneakers
are hard to walk in.

Platforms

Platform sneakers are tall. They have thick soles. The soles can be 1 to 4 inches (2.5 to 10 centimeters) high. They're tall and flat. They give wearers a little height. Platform sneakers are safer than heels. Heels can be shaky. Platform sneakers are more comfortable. They look a little dressy because of the height. But they're still sneakers. So, they can be casual too.

Bella Hadid is a fashion model. She has over 30 million Instagram followers. She loves wearing sneakers. She wears sneakers with everything. She wears sneakers with fancy dresses. She has posted photos wearing many different platform sneakers.

BE A LITTLE
EXTRA

SOCIAL MEDIA CHALLENGE

Throwing sneakers is a social media trend. Some throw sneakers in the air to see how they land. Some throw sneakers "on." They edit their video. They make it look like they suddenly changed clothes and shoes. Make a video to post on TikTok.

Throw sneakers up into the air. Throw them across the room.

Try doing different types of throws.

Try throwing different types of sneakers or shoes.

Film everything. Edit as needed.

Consider putting the video in slow motion.

Add a few hashtags. Maybe use #sneakerchallenge.

Come up with your own social media challenge.

Kendall Jenner is a famous model. During Paris Fashion Week, she wore platform sneakers. She wore these sneakers several times. Her sneakers were **embellished**. Embellished means decorated. Her sneakers had stars.

There are different ways to embellish platform sneakers. Some platform sneakers have cutouts. Some have designs like hearts. Some have crystal beads. Some are **textured**. Textured means having a rough surface.

Platform sneakers are not just for women. They're designed for men as well. They're part of a high fashion **streetwear** look. Streetwear is a casual style. It came from the skateboarding culture. It includes jeans, shirts, and sneakers.

◄ Platforms can be added to shoes, boots, or sandals.

There is see-through luggage.
That's a lot of pressure to pack neatly.

See-through Sneakers

See-through fashion is not new. It's been around in women's fashion. There are see-through heels. There are see-though boots. There are see-through clothes. But fashion is becoming more **gender-fluid**. This means not male or female. See-through fashion is now in menswear.

See-through sneakers are also trendy. These sneakers are made of clear materials. Some sneakers are made with clear plastic. Some are made with **mesh**. Mesh looks like netting. People are able to see the wearers' feet and socks.

Some of these sneakers are totally clear. Some may have solid **panels**. Panels are strips. These panels may be made of different materials. They may be different colors.

Blondey McCoy is a professional skateboarder. He's also a fashion designer. He worked with a big shoe company. He created a new sneaker design. His sneakers are see-through. They're also **vegan**. This means no animals were used to make the sneakers.

Kanye West is a famous rapper. He also designs sneakers. He has almost 4 million Instagram followers. His newest shoe is see-through. It has a lot of open spaces. It's made of **algae**. Algae is a water plant. West wants to protect Earth. He said, "We're going to be farming and going seed to sole."

◄ Many companies, from Nike to PUMA, have released see-through sneakers.

Nike continues to honor Kobe Bryant's legacy
with the Nike Kobe Black Mamba Collection.
Pictured is the 2017 Nike Kobe A.D. Big Stage.

All-White Sneakers

Bold colors and patterns come in and out of style. But all-white sneakers have always been trendy. They've been around for a while. The first sneakers were white. They were mainly **athletic** shoes. Athletes are people who train to play sports.

Today, all-white sneakers are hot. They can be worn with any outfit. They're even worn with suits. Influencers mix white sneakers with clothes of different colors and fabrics. Clothes are more colorful today. This supports a clean footwear look.

There are three things today's sneaker buyers want. Buyers want chunky sneakers. (These are also called "dad shoes" or "ugly dad sneakers.") They want simple sneakers. They want **authentic** sneakers. Authentic means real. All-white sneakers are all of these things. They upgrade casual looks. They look sharp.

Did you know...

- Michael Jordan is a professional basketball player. He's thought to be the best player. He's connected with Nike sneakers. But he wanted to be with Adidas. Nike gave him a better deal.

- Wearing sneakers is a big part of the streetwear look. Alojz Abram is known as "Streetwear Gramps." He's over 70 years old. Jannik is his grandson. He's known as "jaadiee." He posts photos of Abram. He calls himself "personal photographer of Gramps."

- Neymar is a professional soccer player. He's from Brazil. He grew up with little money. As a kid, he could only afford to buy one pair of sneakers. He wore them until they got holes. Today, he's one of the highest-paid athletes. He has over 140 million Instagram followers. He set a record. He bought over $18,000 worth of sneakers.

Sneakers are meant to get scuffed. Colors hide scratches and dirt. All-white shoes get soiled. They're hard to keep clean. Some people are scared of all-white shoes. But influencers make wearing white shoes look easy.

PJ Tucker is a professional basketball player. He is known as the "sneaker king" both on and off the court. He was once spotted wearing a pair of white sneakers that cost over $6,000!

In June 2020, Virgil Abloh helped raise money for the Black Lives Matter movement. He auctioned off a pair of off-white sneakers. It sold for $186,859.49.

▲ The Adidas Stan Smith all-white sneakers are considered an iconic sneaker staple.

Sneakerheads dream of having
sneaker collabs.

Customized Kicks

Sneakers reflect personalities. Sneaker **collabs** are a trend. Collabs are collaborations. They're partnerships. People team up with sneaker companies. They help design sneakers. But it's not just people or celebrities who do collaborations. Even companies do them. Ben & Jerry's partnered with Nike to release an eye-popping, colorful sneaker.

Designing sneakers is not just for famous people and companies. Anyone can do it. **Customizing** means to make something that fits one's personal needs. Customizing kicks is trendy. Sneakers are thought to be "wearable art."

Some shoe companies have custom shops. Buyers can choose colors. They can choose materials. They can choose designs. They can add embellishments.

Another trend is to draw on sneakers. Joshua Vides is a designer and artist. He uses a black marker. He draws on sneakers. He has a comic-book style. His sneakers have sold out. He said, "I simply used the shoes as a canvas." Canvas means a cloth to be painted on. Vides inspired others. People customize their own kicks. They want to have one-of-a-kind sneakers. Some people draw on their sneakers with markers or paints. Some add fabrics. Some sew on designs.

Another way to customize is to rebuild sneakers. People take sneakers apart. They put sneakers back together. But they use different materials.

◄ People want to bring attention to their sneakers.

Teenagers can raid their parents'
closets to find **throwback** fashion gems.
Throwbacks are reminders of the past.

Sneaker Comebacks

Fashion trends from the past are trendy again. This is called **nostalgic** fashion. Nostalgia is a longing for the past. It's also called **retro** fashion. Retro means going back in time. People find comfort in trends from the past. They find it familiar. They find it safe. Specifically, fashion from the 1980s, 1990s, and 2000s is coming back.

Many shoe companies are doing retro releases. These companies are bringing back old sneakers. They're reselling them.

Some retro styles are coming back. There are many examples. The "no laces" look is back. This means Velcro strap sneakers are in. Velcro is strips that stick together.

THROWBACK

OG INFLUENCER

There were influencers before social media. An original (or "OG") sneakers influencer was Chuck Taylor. Taylor lived from 1901 to 1969. He was a professional basketball player. But he's more famous for his sneakers. Converse is a shoe company. In 1917, it made the All Star basketball sneakers. These sneakers were the world's first high-tops. Taylor shared design tips with Converse. He made the sneakers more flexible. He added more support. His design has been the same for over 90 years. In 1921, Taylor endorsed the sneakers. He was the first celebrity to do so. He signed his name on the star logo. The shoes are called Chuck Taylor All Stars. They're called Chuck Taylors, for short. Taylor promoted the sneakers. He traveled around the country. He went to games. He went to stores. For many years, his shoes were the official sneakers of basketball players. During World War II, Taylor served as a captain in the U.S. Air Force. Soldiers trained in his shoes. Chuck Taylors are the all-time best-selling sneakers.

Dad shoes are super popular. They're chunky. They're oversized. They come in soft tones. They're comfortable. They're practical. They're part of a **normcore** look. Normcore means normal-looking clothes. It's stylish and relaxed. It includes jeans, shirts, sweats, socks, and sneakers.

Dad shoes are often called ugly. But designers and influencers have embraced the ugliness. They've made them trendy. For example, Leo Mandella is an influencer. He's known as "Gully GuyLeo." He has over 705,000 followers. He wears a lot of dad shoes. He also wore them at the men's Fashion Week in Paris.

▲ White and black socks are often worn with dad shoes.

Glossary

algae (AL-jee) water plant

athletic (ath-LET-ik) related to sports

authentic (aw-THEN-tik) real, genuine

canvas (KAN-vuhs) cloth that is painted on

collabs (kuh-LABZ) collaborations or partnerships

customizing (KUHS-tuh-mize-ing) changing in order to fit one's style

dominate (DAH-muh-nate) to rule over

embellished (em-BEL-ishd) decorated to add beauty

following (FAH-loh-ing) fans or supporters

gender-fluid (JEN-dur FLOO-id) not restricted to being male or female

influencers (IN-floo-uhns-urz) people who set trends by posting a lot on social media and have large followings

mesh (MESH) netting

normcore (NORM-kor) style that is meant to look average or basic

nostalgic (nah-STAL-jik) having a longing for the past

panels (PAN-uhlz) solid strips

retro (RET-roh) going back in time

social media (SOH-shuhl MEE-dee-uh) online communications used to share information

soles (SOHLZ) bottoms of shoes

streetwear (STREET-wair) a casual style that comes from skateboarding culture and that includes jeans, shirts, and sneakers

textured (TEKS-churd) having a rough surface

throwback (THROH-bak) reminder of the past

trending (TREND-ing) currently a popular fad online

vegan (VEE-guhn) a person who doesn't eat or use animal products

Learn More

Keyser, Amber J. *Sneaker Century: A History of Athletic Shoes*. Minneapolis, MN: Lerner Publishing Group, 2015.

Knight, Phil. *Shoe Dog: Young Readers Edition*. New York, NY: Simon & Schuster Books for Young Readers, 2017.

Loh-Hagan, Virginia. *Far Out Fashion*. Ann Arbor, MI: Cherry Lake Publishing, 2018.

Index